GREAT MINECRAFT® BUILDS

YOUR UNOFFICIAL GUIDE TO

BUILDING COOL MINECRAFT® FARMS

S. D. MORISON

Enslow PUBLISHING

Please visit our website, www.enslow.com. For a free color catalog of all our high-quality books, call toll free 1-800-398-2504 or fax 1-877-980-4454.

Cataloging-in-Publication Data
Names: Morison, S. D.
Title: Your unofficial guide to building cool Minecraft® farms / S. D. Morison.
Description: New York : Enslow Publishing, 2023. | Series: Great Minecraft® builds | Includes glossary and index.
Identifiers: ISBN 9781978529304 (pbk.) | ISBN 9781978529328 (library bound) | ISBN 9781978529311 (6pack) | ISBN 9781978529335 (ebook)
Subjects: LCSH: Minecraft (Game)--Juvenile literature. | Farms--Juvenile literature.
| Building--Juvenile literature.
Classification: LCC GV1469.35.M535 M672 2023 | DDC 794.8--dc23

Published in 2023 by
Enslow Publishing
29 E. 21st Street
New York, NY 10010

Portions of this work were originally authored by Jill Keppeler and published as *The Unofficial Guide to Building Farms in Minecraft.* All new material this edition authored by S. D. Morison.

Designer: Rachel Rising
Editor: Jill Keppeler
Illustrator: Matías Lapegüe

Photo credits: Cover, pp. 1-4, ,6 8, 10, 12, 14, 16, 18, 20, 22-24 Orange Sky ART/Shutterstock.com; Cover, pp. 1-24 Phoenix 1319/ Shutterstock.com; Cover, pp. 1, 3, 6, 8, 10, 12, 14, 16, 18, 20, 22-24 Soloma/Shutterstock.com; pp. 1, 3, 6, 8, 10, 12, 14, 16, 18, 20 Phoenix 1319/Shutterstock.com; p. 4 A.Hixon/Shutterstock.com; p. 19 Alexey Laputin/Shutterstock.com.

Printed in the United States of America

CPSIA compliance information: Batch #CSENS23: For further information contact Enslow Publishing, New York, New York, at 1-800-398-2504.

CONTENTS

Words in the glossary appear in **bold** type the first time they are used in the text.

CARING FOR THE LAND

Farms are important! They produce food for people around the world. People who run farms in the real world work hard to care for the land and grow things to feed us all. And in *Minecraft*, farms can also help your character, your friends' characters, and helpful *Minecraft* mobs.

Minecraft farming is simpler in many ways than real-world farming, but there are still things to know and learn to make the best farm you can. You can also learn a few things about how things work in real farms.

In *Minecraft's* survival mode, you need to eat to stay healthy and keeping playing. Farming will help you get food. Eating food items gives you back hunger points in *Minecraft*.

WHAT TO GROW?

One reason to make a *Minecraft* farm is to grow crops. There are a number of different crops in the game. They include wheat, carrots, potatoes, beetroots, melons, and pumpkins. There are also other plants that will produce things you can use in making things to eat.

Some plants grow wild. Some can be found in village farms. You need seeds to grow wheat, beets, melons, or pumpkins. You can get wheat or beetroot seeds by chopping at *Minecraft* grass. Villages also can have farms or chests where you can get seeds.

ADVENTURE MODE

Plant a carrot or potato to grow more of them. You can do the same with sweet berries found growing wild.

The plant shown here is sugarcane. You can't eat it, but you can use it to make sugar to use in other things. It needs to be planted next to water.

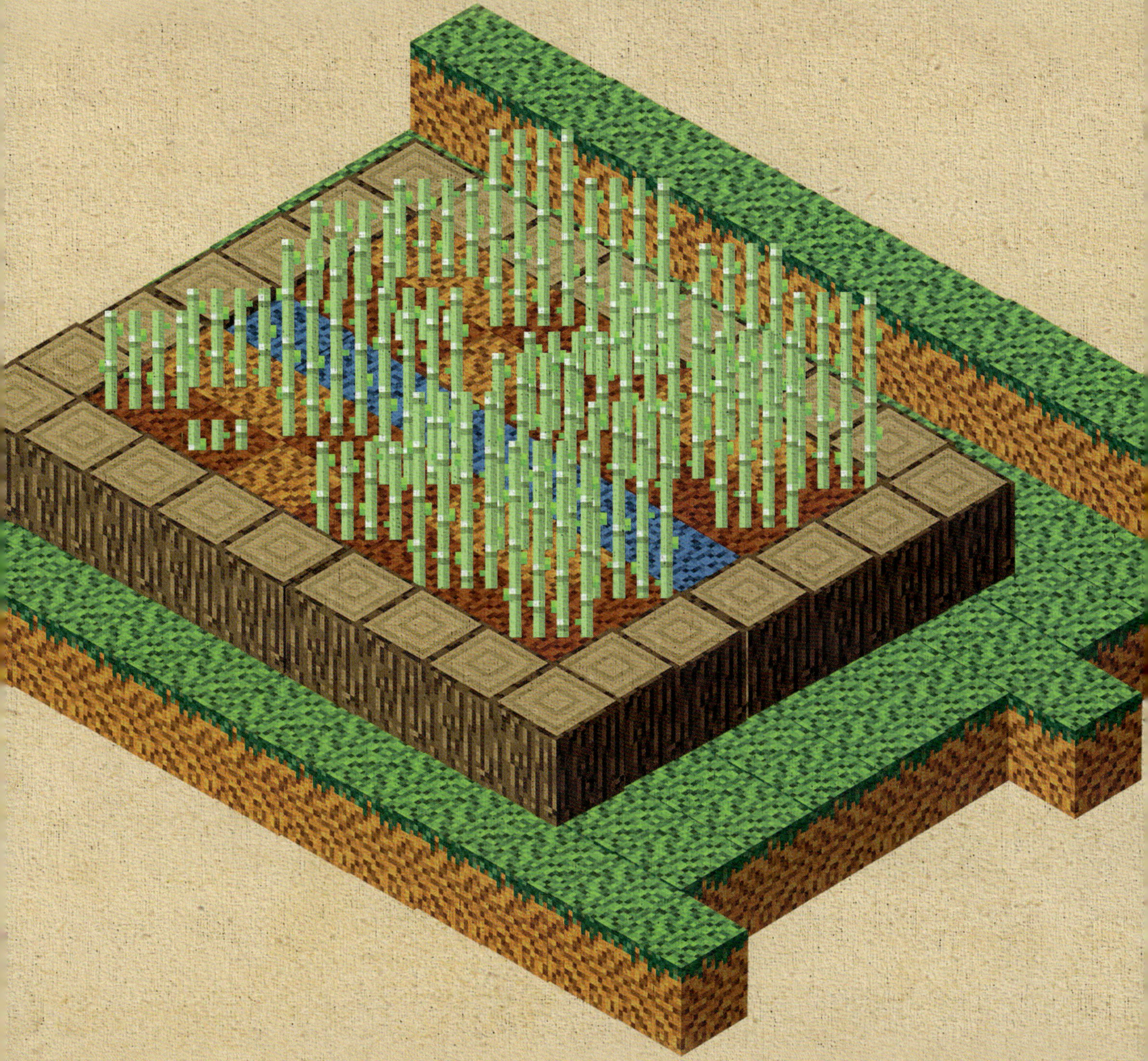

TOOLS AND FARMLAND

Crops need farmland to grow on. To make farmland, you need to craft a hoe using items and a crafting table. Then use the hoe on a block of dirt or grass. However, your farmland block will soon change back to regular dirt if you don't plant something in it or **hydrate** it!

To hydrate farmland, there must be water at least four blocks away on the same level or one level above. The water can be flowing or still. Rain can also hydrate farmland, but this won't last.

ADVENTURE MODE

A few plants won't grow on farmland. These include sweet berries, sugarcane, and mushrooms (although these are **fungi**). Others will but don't need it.

It will take varying amounts of time for farmland to fully hydrate. A fully hydrated block of farmland will be deep brown.

PLOTTING IT OUT

Crops on hydrated farmland often grow faster. There are many different ways to create a good farm plot. You can have a plot that's nine blocks by nine blocks with a single water block in the middle. Or you can have a plot with pathways that let you walk through your crops or one that's raised above the ground.

Remember that melons and pumpkins grow in a different way from other *Minecraft* crops. They need two blocks each. A stalk grows from their seeds, and a pumpkin or melon grows from the stalk.

ADVENTURE MODE

To carry water in *Minecraft*, you need a bucket, which takes three iron **ingots**. If you don't have one, you can plant your crops at the edge of a natural body of water.

In addition to hydration, other things can affect the growth of your crops as well. They need light, and a player needs to be within a certain range.

BE PATIENT

After you plant your crops, you have to wait, unless you use bone meal (made, of course, from bones) on them. This will speed growth up, although you may still have some waiting to do depending on the crop.

Minecraft crops will look different depending on what stage they're in. If you try to **harvest** them too early, you won't get anything new! Wheat can be harvested when it's a darker green-brown. Vegetables are done growing when you can see their tops. You won't see pumpkins or melons at all until they're grown.

ADVENTURE MODE

Harvesting some crops will also give you seeds for them. Harvesting melons will give you slices of melon. Harvesting pumpkins, potatoes, and carrots will give you more of the same crop.

As with sugarcane, you can't directly eat *Minecraft* wheat. It's something you can use in other things. You can directly eat other crops, but they can also be used in other recipes too.

SIMPLE ... OR NOT!

While farming in *Minecraft* can be quite simple—just a few crops to give you some food and supplies—it doesn't have to be. Some players build big, **complicated** farms, with minecarts to help them move crops.

You can also use redstone to help you build machines to **automatically** harvest crops. Some farm **designs** use water to flood the ground. This can send the plants to a hopper, or a device that collects them. Some designs use *Minecraft* **pistons**. This isn't always the most **efficient** way to do things, though. See what works for you!

ADVENTURE MODE

Redstone dust comes from mining redstone ore. It helps to move redstone power, which is much like electricity.

With redstone, you power minecarts to move on their own. You can also power pistons and other machines.

OTHER KINDS OF FARMS

People usually think of farms as producing plants we can eat. This is true, but farms can also produce other kinds of **resources**. This is also the case in *Minecraft*. The game's livestock include cows, pigs, chickens, and sheep. You can get meat from each of these animals. You can also get other resources such as wool, eggs, feathers, milk, and leather.

You can raise horses, mules, and donkeys in *Minecraft*. Other passive or neutral mobs that can provide resources include bees, mooshrooms, rabbits, goats, and llamas.

ADVENTURE MODE

A mooshroom is a *Minecraft* mob that is like a cow covered in mushrooms. They only appear in mushroom fields **biomes**.

In *Minecraft*, a passive mob is one that will never attack the player. These include cows and most other livestock mobs. A neutral mob may attack the player in certain cases.

HELPFUL FARM MOBS

Bees are neutral mobs and can't be tamed. However, they can be helpful in *Minecraft*. They are attracted, or drawn to, flowers or berry bushes and can **pollinate** many plants, including crops. That can make those plants grow faster. They also make honey, which players can collect from bee nests and beehives and use for food.

You can get milk from cows, mooshrooms, and goats if you have a bucket. Milk can be used in recipes. If you drink it, it will remove status effects in *Minecraft*, such as those from **potions** or poisons.

ADVENTURE MODE

You can naturally find bee nests in trees in some *Minecraft* biomes. You can make beehives with wood planks and honeycomb from bee nests.

Bees won't attack you unless you attack them or their nest or if you take honey from their nest or hive. In *Minecraft*, build a campfire under the nest to prevent this.

A HAPPY HOME

In real life, farming made it so people could settle down in one place instead of always traveling. This is true in *Minecraft* too. You can build a base and have resources there so you don't always have to search for them.

If you replant, crops will keep growing as you harvest them. You can also breed livestock animals, or cause them to make baby animals, if you feed them certain things. If you take care, your *Minecraft* farm can help you with resources for a long time!

ADVENTURE MODE

It will take baby animals about 20 minutes to grow up in a *Minecraft* game.

Different crops will help you draw different livestock to your farm—and also to breed them. Try seeds, wheat, carrots, potatoes, and beetroots!

GLOSSARY

automatically Happening on its own, without being directly controlled.

biome A natural community of plants and animals, such as a forest or desert.

complicated Hard to explain or understand, or having many parts.

design The pattern or shape of something. Also, to create the pattern or shape of something.

efficient Capable of producing desired results without wasting results, time, or energy.

fungus A living thing that's like a plant but that doesn't have leaves, flowers, or green color or make its own food. The plural form is fungi.

harvest To gather crops after they've grown.

hydrate To add water to something.

ingot A piece of metal formed into a shape, such as a brick.

piston A sliding piece that's part of a machine.

pollinate To take pollen from one flower, plant, or tree to another.

potion A mixture of liquids.

resource Something that can be used.

FOR MORE INFORMATION

BOOKS

Castaldo, Nancy, and Ginnie Hsu. *The Farm That Feeds Us.* Words and Pictures, 2020.
Miller, Megan. *Minecraft Engineer: Incredible Starter Farms.* New York, New York: Sky Pony Press, 2018.
Mojang AB. *Minecraft Guide to Farming*. New York, NY: Del Rey, 2017.

WEBSITES

Instructables: Farming in Minecraft
www.instructables.com/Farming-in-Minecraft/
This website has a step-by-step look at starting to farm in *Minecraft.*

Minecraft Wiki: Farming
minecraft.fandom.com/wiki/Farming
This website has an in-depth look at farming in *Minecraft.*

Tutorial: Bedrock Beginner Farms
www.minecraft.net/en-us/article/tutorial–bedrock-beginner-farms
A video tutorial to making efficient *Minecraft* farms.

INDEX